an easy-read ACTIVITY book

MAKING UFOs

written and illustrated by

DAVE ROSS

A GROLIER COMPANY

Franklin Watts
New York | London | Toronto | Sydney
1980

To Paulie and Donnie

R.L. 3.2 Spache Revised Formula

Library of Congress Cataloging in Publication Data

Ross, Dave
  Making UFOs.

  (An Easy-read activity book)
  SUMMARY: Contains directions for making UFOs
from materials found around the house.
  1. Unidentified flying objects — Models — Juvenile
literature. [1. Unidentified flying objects — Models.
2. Handicraft] I. Title.
TL789.R67   001.9′42′0228   80-11305
ISBN 0-531-04144-1

CONTENTS

UFO stands for **U**nidentified **F**lying **O**bject. There have been reports of UFO sightings all around the world. Even people who lived hundreds of years ago wrote about seeing strange things in the sky.

People say they have seen UFOs in many different sizes and shapes. Some people believe that UFOs are ships from outer space.

This book shows you how to make your own UFOs from things you can find around the house. The pictures in the book show some of the ways to make UFOs. Find new materials. Use old materials in new ways. Try to make your UFOs better than mine!

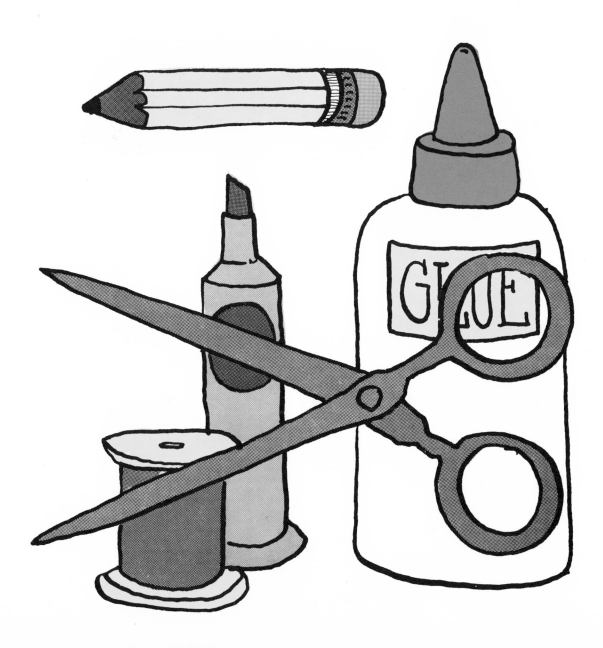

A UFO YOU CAN FLY!

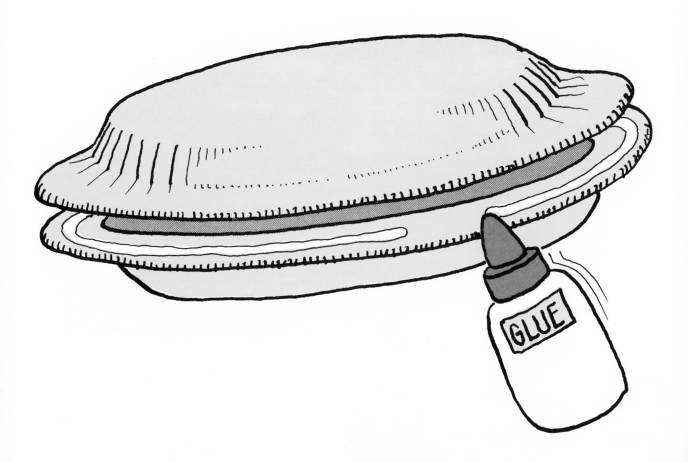

You will need two paper plates for this simple
UFO.

Tape or glue the plates together. Be sure to
let the glue dry. Then launch your UFO!

Some other ideas

1. Draw UFO designs on the outside with crayons or magic markers.

2. Cut a hatch in the top and make an alien who peeks out.

3. Have a UFO flying contest with your friends.

TURN A SMALL BOX INTO A UFO

Start with a small box. Ask a grown-up to help you cut slots in the sides.

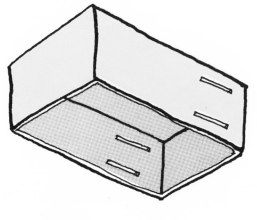

Make wings and fins from flat sticks or cardboard.

Push these through the slots and tape them on the inside.

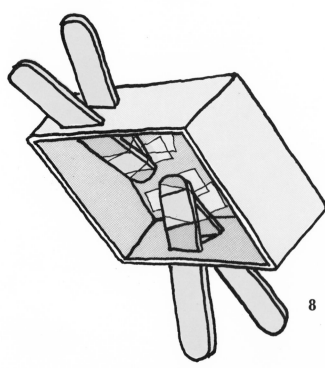

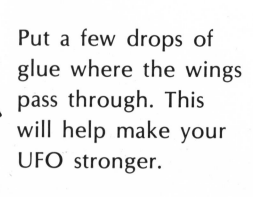

Put a few drops of glue where the wings pass through. This will help make your UFO stronger.

8

Glue rockets on the
ends of the wings.
You can make
rockets from old
lipstick tubes or
toothpaste caps.

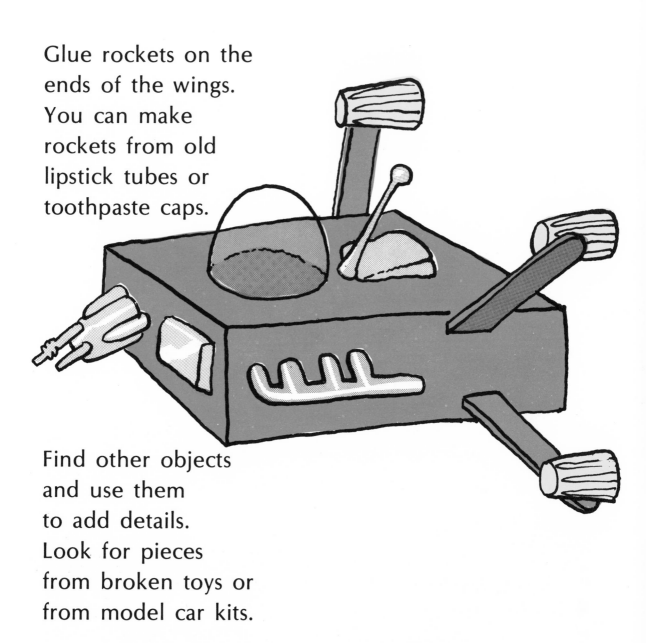

Find other objects
and use them
to add details.
Look for pieces
from broken toys or
from model car kits.

Let the glue dry and
then paint your UFO.

DRAWING UFOs

All you will need are paper and pencil. But you can use magic markers, crayons, paints, or pencils to add decoration.

Start by drawing a shape
If you draw the shape freehand, it can be squiggly.

If you use a ruler, it will have straight edges. You can use jar lids to trace round shapes.

Try all three shapes together. Draw the shapes large enough so you can add lots of details.

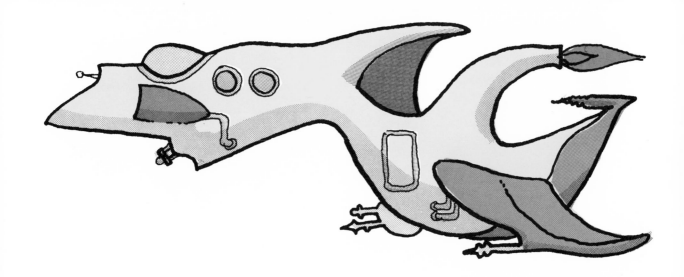

Drawing the Outside

Cut out the UFO and paste it on a piece of paper. Use crayons or markers for the background. Shade the edges to make them look round.

Some other ideas

1. Show the same UFO from the top, sides, and front.

2. Make a whole group of UFOs.

3. Draw a picture of a UFO landing—maybe near your own house!

4. Try drawing some of these: a space ark, space freighter, mining ship, battle ship, fighter space pirate, imperial cruiser, deep-space explorer.

11

Drawing the Inside

When you draw the inside of a UFO, think about showing some of these things: control rooms, crew quarters, passageways, galleys, engine rooms, computer rooms, machinery, and tools.

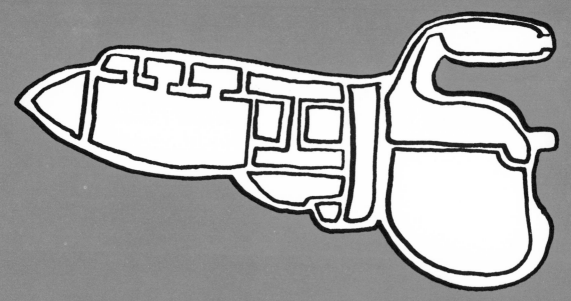

Some other ideas
1. Make the rooms out of pieces of paper and fit them together.
2. Cut the UFO shape out of cardboard and hang it from the ceiling.
3. Make drawings of aliens who could fly your UFO.

MAKING TINY UFOs

split pea

bottle cap

thumbtack, or drawing pin

cork covered with foil

fins cut from paper

broken toothpicks

pins stuck in cork

part of a ball-point pen

pipe cleaner

flame cut out of paper

magic marker cap

portholes cut out of paper with a paper punch

plastic bottle cap

fishing bobber, or cork

HOW TO DISPLAY TINY UFOs

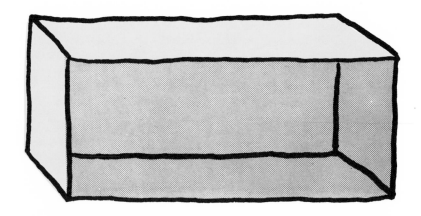

Start with a small box or carton.

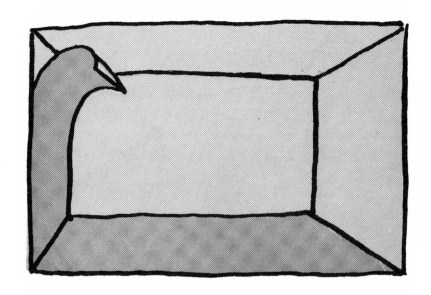

Glue pieces of paper inside the box.

Cut planets, stars, and moons out of paper and paste them on the background.

Make the bottom into the surface of a planet by gluing sand, dirt, or small stones onto a piece of crumpled-up paper.

Glue or tie the UFOs to pieces of thread and hang them from the top of the box.

UFOs MADE FROM PICNIC SUPPLIES

You will need
a paper or styrofoam drinking cup
three plastic forks
a piece of paper
scissors
tape or glue

For wings
Cut out three squares
the same size. Fold
them from corner to
corner. Fold the
edges back.

For a nose cone
Trace something
round to make a
circle and cut out
the circle. Cut the
circle in half.

Pull the ends of
your half circle
together and fasten
with glue or tape.

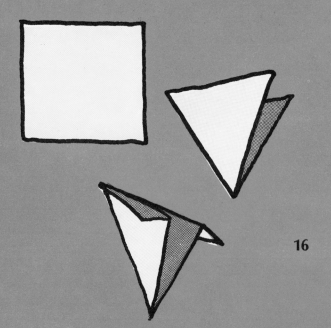

16

Glue the nose cone and wings on the UFO.

Tape or glue the forks on the
inside of the cup. This is the
landing gear.

Paint the outside
with magic markers.
Or you can glue on
things that you have
cut from paper.

MAKE A PAPIER-MÂCHÉ UFO

Find a good shape
for your UFO.
(Plastic bottles
work well.)

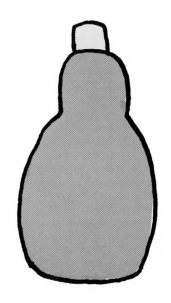

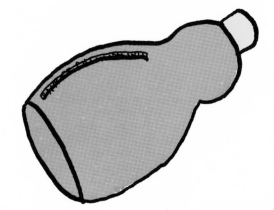

Ask someone to
help you make slots
in the sides
for wings.

Cut the wings
out of cardboard
and tape them on.

Tape other shapes
on the bottle.

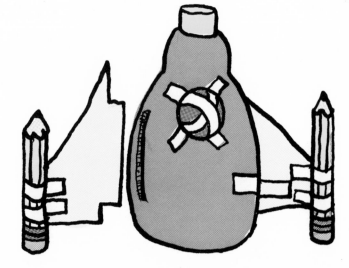

To make a papier-mâché mix
Use one cup of wallpaper paste mixed with two cups of water. Or boil one cup of white flour with two cups of water.

Dip strips of newspaper into the mix and squeeze off the extra paste. Cover the whole UFO shape by crossing the strips in different directions.

Let the UFO dry overnight before painting.

Paint portholes and hatches on the UFO.
You can also add stripes and symbols.

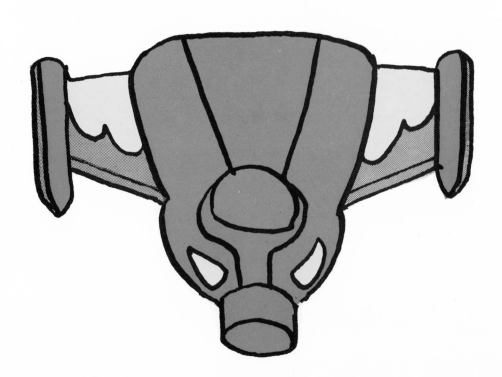

You can add other things, too. Poke nails, screws, or golf tees into the covered shape. Don't leave any sharp edges sticking out!

You can glue on parts of model kits or pieces from old board games. Look around the house and see what other things you can find!

GOGGLES FOR UFO SIGHTINGS

You will need
a strip of paper 24 inches (61 cm) long
    and 3 inches (7.6 cm) wide
pipe cleaners
cellophane
markers or crayons
scissors

Cut a notch in the middle of the strip and make holes for your eyes.

Tape the cellophane over the eye openings.
Use pipe cleaners to make the antennas.

Draw designs on the other side.

Ask someone to help tape the ends
together so the goggles will fit your head.

A SINGLE-SEAT UFO

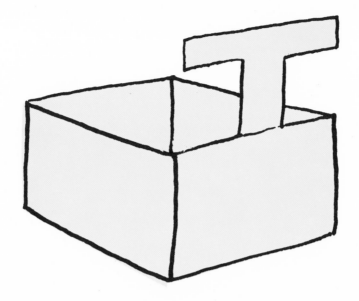

Start with a cardboard box. Ask a grown-up to help you cut off all the top flaps except for one. Cut that one in the shape of a T. It will be the front of your UFO.

To make fins, tape the cut-off flaps to the bottom of the box.

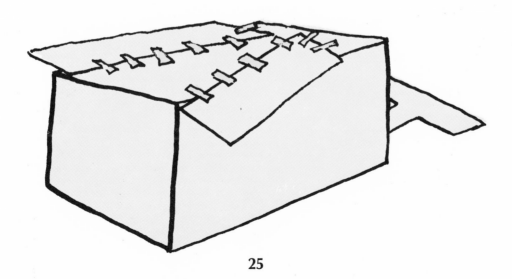

IDEAS FOR INSIDE A SINGLE-SEAT UFO

Make a control panel from bottle caps or buttons.

Fasten paper cups on the back for rockets.

Paint on UFO designs.

Cut portholes out of heavy paper or cardboard.

A UFO-SCOPE

You will need
a cardboard tube
a piece of cellophane

a rubber band
paper and a pencil
scissors

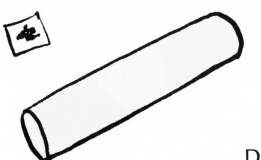

Draw a small UFO on
the paper. Cut it out and
glue it to the cellophane.
Put the cellophane on the
end of the tube and fasten
it with a rubber band.

UFO HELMET

You will need a large plastic bottle. A big milk or water bottle works well. Rinse it out. Ask someone to help you cut off the bottom of the bottle.

Put the bottle over your head and ask someone to mark where you should cut openings for your eyes.

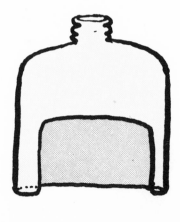

You can make the blast shield from another
piece of plastic. Then get two paper fasteners
to attach the shield to the helmet. This will
let the shield move up and down.

Punch a hole on each side of the bottom.
Fasten a piece of string through and you will
be able to keep the helmet on.

Decorate your helmet with details made from
cut paper or pipe cleaners. Or draw designs
on the helmet with magic markers.

TURN YOUR ROOM INTO A UFO!

Get a piece of paper big enough to cover a window. Cut a circle out of the paper for a porthole. Tape the paper over the window.

Cover two chairs with a blanket to make an escape craft.

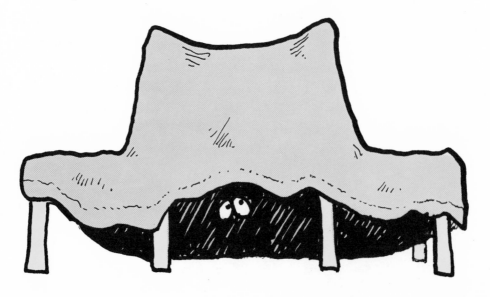

Make rocket controls out of a cardboard box. Use a stick or broom handle with a thumbtack in the end.

Cut dials out of white paper. Draw numbers and needles with a marker or crayon. Glue them on the outside of the box.

HAVE A UFO ADVENTURE

Be sure to take along enough food for
your trip:

a thermos full of milk
a sandwich
   (wrapped carefully to avoid space dust)
a piece of fruit
a piece of cake
a chocolate bar
   (for energy)

Other things you may need
a battery light (to signal)
paper and pencil (to draw pictures of
   everything you see on your trip)
a transistor radio (static is a good UFO noise)